3 GREATEST TRAPS THAT KEEP YOU CHASING MONEY, INSTEAD OF MAKING MONEY TO CREATE THE LIFE YOU DREAM

CHRIS VAUGHN

Copyright © 2018 by Chris Vaughn

All rights reserved.

All rights reserved. Except as permitted under the U.S. Copyright Act of 1976, no part of this publication may be reproduced, distributed, or transmitted in any form or by any means, or stored in a database or retrieval system, without the prior written permission of the author/publisher.

No part of this book may be reproduced in any form or by any electronic or mechanical means, including information storage and retrieval systems, without written permission from the author, except for the use of brief quotations in a book review.

Good Lord Publishing 2890-A Georgia Highway 212 #123 Conyers, GA 30094

 Created with Vellum

3 Greatest Traps that Keep you Chasing Money, Instead of Making Money to Create the Life you Dream

First Edition: March 2018

Vaughn, Chris (2018-03-26).

Good Lord Publishing Kindle & Paperback Edition.

DEDICATION

To my wife Lisa, who has always encouraged me to chase my dreams, and to write those dreams down.

To SB, MA, and LC for giving life longevity and meaning.

To my Daddy and Mama.
One gave me the strength of convictions, thanks Daddy; one gifted me with the ability to tell a story, thanks Mama.

PSALMS 1:1-3 (ESV)

1 Blessed is the man who walks not in the counsel of the wicked, nor stands in the way of sinners, nor sits in the seat of scoffers; **2** but his delight is in the law of the Lord, and on his law he meditates day and night. **3** He is like a tree planted by streams of water that yields its fruit in its season, and its leaf does not wither. In all that he does, he prospers.

THEY ASKED, "NOW WHAT?"

A few months back I'm lurking on social media and in Facebook Groups just reading and seeing where people are at and what they are dealing with in creating their online business, and just being an entrepreneur.

Post after post were encouraging people to sign up to different programs, webinars, and such as well as all the 'tools of the trade' that we use or plan to use as we pursue our entrepreneurial dreams. Then I ran across this one post that hit me hard! I'm just using blank all cap placeholders for the companies they had signed up to, but they wrote:

"I've signed up to EMAIL AUTOMATION COMPANY and also to LANDING PAGE BUILDER, and also to MARKETING WIDGETS... now what?"

I honestly hurt inside for them!

I know what those programs cost which meant they had paid out somewhere between $800 to $2000 for either a Bronze package, or the Silver package of each product. Who knows, they may have gone all out and bought the Gold packages for all three of the products and spent $4000+!

But the part of the comment that screamed out to me was, **"NOW WHAT?"**

They are like so many people who dream of financial independence.

They are tired of where they are financially?

Caught up in the rat race that always finds them running in circles?

They find themselves at the end of the month, with still more month of bills than they have money.

Truly we've all been there. And we all want to get to the place of financial independence. To end a month with more money that we started with and the ability to create the life we want, and to live the life we dream.

Since you are reading this, I'm sure you have dreams you want to see come to pass. Hopes that are yet fulfilled. And like so many, bills that need to be paid.

WHAT A DAY WE LIVE IN!

We live in the greatest day of human history. I've said countless times the Internet is the greatest human invention ever conceived, and barely second is the Smart Phone. Everyone has within their hands the power to discover, access, and harness an almost unlimited amount of knowledge, and even better, opportunities.

At the time of writing this, I typed into Google, "income opportunities" and there are 198,000,000+ results. WOW! Almost 200 MILLION searchable opportunities available to everyone at this moment to increase their income!

Now I don't believe that all of those opportunities are valid, good, or even a fit for me, or you. But if only **ONE MILLIONETH** or 1% of 1% of 1% were great opportunities... that would still leave 198 opportunities available for someone to utilize to help create the life they want, and the financial independence they dream of, and the security in life they crave.

The problem with most people isn't the selection of an opportunity, but the fact there are too many.

For so many people there is a new endeavor from last year, and new launch last month, or even the next best thing last week. And like a hamster on a wheel, they are spinning their wheels, chasing their dreams but at the end of each night coming up empty.

Sadly they are not only losing resources from their life, but wasting the one commodity that everyone has in common.

The one commodity no one can save.

The only commodity that is spent as fast as it comes into our lives.

Those people are losing the resource of TIME!

I have a friend who I believe has been a part of every multi-level business or start-up opportunity that comes his way. Every time we talk he begins to tell me about his **'NEW'** opportunity and how it's going to make him rich, and let him quit his job. Again, I mean EVERY TIME I see him it's something new. One time it was specialized painting on ceilings of star patterns. Another time it was next best weight loss system, and he's done several of those. So many other times it's the next and greatest multi-level program to get a commission on everyone's online purchases (which you can do through an Affiliate program and you don't have to pay an upfront fee to do it but that is another topic we can explore later). And guess what? He keeps wasting time, spending money, and chasing money; INSTEAD OF MAKING MONEY!

Do you want to be like that constantly spending money and resources of time and not getting anywhere? Or do you want to see your dreams come true, creating a business that builds you an income in the process.

Now with the power of the internet there are so many more opportunities.... At least 198! And better yet, you can at the drop of a hat, and the push of a play button on a web page or podcast player hear so many great Online Entrepreneurs that are making a difference in people's lives offering training, programs, and resources! I love them! I'm thankful for them and the knowledge they share, but it's sometimes **information overload** and too easy to get caught up in the hamster wheel and start chasing the wrong things.

Some online entrepreneurs instead of working towards their dreams, get caught up in the next system of mechanics, the next sales funnel, the next automated email service, and while they chase and spend money they don't have, for things and programs that they don't need or know how to implement, but are convinced that they need to have this NEW THING **'right now'?**

- Click Funnels.
- Drip.
- LeadPages.
- Kajabi.
- SamCart.
- HostGator.
- Evernote.
- PopUp Ally.
- Canva.
- 1Password.
- Hootsuite.
- Drip.
- Bluehost.

- ConvertKit.
- Not to mention so many other webinars, courses, programs, Masterminds, etc. that are out there.

Every one of those listed above are GREAT PRODUCTS! Some I use, some I don't, and some I will, and some I'll never use; but not one of those products, programs, courses, etc. will do the one thing you or I want... None directly create an **active income** or a **passive income**. They all can be great tools to utilize in the process of building your business, developing your email list, webinars, copy writing, and creating the income you desire, but you have to remember the old adage:

When your outgo, is more than your income, your upkeep will be your downfall!

Bootstrap Business Academy is focused on helping you start the business that's in your heart to achieve the life you want to create!

We've all been there I think. And especially when you are in a place in life where you need every extra dime just to make your house note, buy groceries, pay off a college loan or even buy gas for your car. Have you ever dug for change in your car to meet a need? I have!

The good news is you don't have to fall into those traps and make those mistakes! That's why **Bootstrap Business Academy** is here!

So let's get into the **THREE TRAPS** that so many fall into causing them to chase money and not create the business and make the money they need that creates the life you desire and helps you to fulfill the hope of your future.

TRAP #1: MISPLACED GOALS

Having misplaced goals is almost as bad as not having any goals.

I don't want to even delve into the thought that as you read this you might say, "I don't have any goals." That's all a whole topic in and of itself! I believe since you are reading this you have goals, but let's uncover that a bit.

Misplaced goals are true goals, but they don't move you specifically to create and leverage where you are, in an applied process to help you achieve specifically what or where you are going after.

Some time back I met a number of online entrepreneurs in a great Facebook group. Their **only stated** goal was to create a large social media footprint. Honestly I got caught up into myself. How many followers do you have on Instagram? Twitter? Facebook? And while a social following does help create online authority, followers in and of themselves do not create any income.

Even if you have 10,000 followers on every social

media platform available, those followers are worthless unless they connect with you, your brand, your mission, etc. and work with your business.

I started watching these guys and gals posting about each new thousand threshold of followers they were getting each week. I utilized their strategies, and I too started getting more and more followers but I then started to sit back and watch their feeds.

- Nothing posted specifically to build a business.
- Nothing that engaged an audience.
- Nothing that would create a product or business.
- Nothing but followers...

Having an active online presence, a noticeable foot print in social media, engagement with others is great, but if your desire is to create either active income or passive income, just having a following of numbers will only get you chasing a popularity contest that never creates anything substantial.

But everyone of those guys in that group achieved their goal.... To have a large social following! But there was no end game. No SPECIFIC GOAL to take them closer to their desired end result.

THAT'S A MISPLACED GOAL!

A misplaced goal is an achievable goal, and possibly a good goal, but misses the mark of moving you closer to your desired destination.

Their goal should have been to create an online community where they could serve people with whatever product or service they were creating that would impact and change their customer's lives for the better. NOPE... they had followers. All that time wasted and MONEY they said they spent for software and apps to create followers wasted and not one step closer to their goal.

Thankfully, I've always been a hacker at heart, so I didn't do all they had done, I just used a couple of their tactics and achieved success to see if their systems worked, and they did, but for me I wanted something more. I want to go in the direction of my goals! Don't you?

Another MISPLACED GOAL is when you are doing whatever you are doing because: IT'S WHAT EVERYONE IS DOING NOW!

When did being a face in the crowd ever create anything but a sense of just being a part of the 'in' group? "We're doing what BIG NAME THOUGHT LEADER is doing now, because it's what EVERYONE is doing!" Is sitting at the popular table going to move you in the direction of your goals?

You know something about misplaced goals; **a misplaced goal will give you a temporary sense of accomplishment, but a long term sense of displacement.** And when you get to the finish line of that goal, you'll wonder, "Why did I want to get here?"

What are your specific goals? Or better yet,

- Where do you want to be in 10 years?
- Where do you want to be in 18 months?
- Where do you want to be in 3 months?

And in that question, we are only dealing with the specific goals of your desire to create a business that can fuel your life.

I'm asking again, "What are your **SPECIFIC** goals?"

And you should have SPECIFIC GOALS:

LONG TERM (5 to 10 years)

MID-RANGE (9 to 18 months)

SHORT-SPECIFIC (4 weeks to 3 months)

Even DAILY GOALS!

The SMART system for goals goes as:

S – Specific

M – Motivating

A – Actionable

R – Realistic but Challenging

T - Trackable

It's a simple system to start getting your life, business, and dreams on paper and on track to be implemented.

Use the space below and let yourself think and dream through your hopes and create SPECIFIC goals RIGHT NOW that will help guide you in the course you are about to set out on. Better yet, get your Journal (Do you have one?) and copy them there so that you can look at them DAILY and be reminded:

My LONG – TERM GOALS (5 to 10 years) are:

_____
_____
_____
_____
_____
_____
_____

_____
_____
_____
_____
_____
_____
_____
_____

Make it a positive affirmation that you speak out such as:

In the next _____ years, I will be experiencing _____ in my life.

In the next _____ years, I will me making _____ per month in revenue, from _____ products that I have created.

In the next _____ years, I will spend _____ hours/weeks/months with my family in our dream vacation.

Better yet, write out your own **specific goal affirmations.**

Take your LONG RANGE goals and break them down further! This will take some time but make the effort and you'll be amazed at the difference it will make in your life.

My MID-RANGE (9 to 18 months) goals are:

_____
_____
_____
_____
_____
_____
_____
_____
_____
_____
_____
_____
_____
_____
_____
_____

TAKE YOUR MID-TERM GOALS AND BREAK THEM down further! What will you accomplish in the next 4 weeks! This is where the details and specifics will you stay the course.

My SHORT-SPECIFIC (4 weeks to 3 months) are:

_____
_____
_____
_____
_____
_____
_____
_____

TRAP #2: CONFUSED VALUES

Your values, or convictions, guide the decisions you make, the people you associate with, and the money you spend!

There is an old adage

> ***It is easier to fall for anything than to stand for something.***

That is completely true and applicable when it comes to business! Your values will determine how you'll treat your business. How you treat your customers? How you handle your competitors? How you'll relate to your family? EVERYTHING in life is a direct result of the values you have, and the actions you take based on those values.

If your values are confused as to why you are doing what you are doing, you will keep doing things that take you off your goals, because your values aren't crystal clear!

An example is the friend of mine who chases every

money making opportunity that comes along. What does he value? ~~Getting rich quick!~~ That's it! All she wrote!

How do I know this? Because as far as I know he's never remained in one business for more than six months. And while I applaud him for making an effort, his actions makes his values crystal clear... his value of commitment is very weak when it comes to making an opportunity work.

If you value your family... you'll make time! Give them a home! Provide warmth and compassion and a safe place to live and grow. If you don't, you won't, and you'll make excuses for why you aren't where you desire to be in life.

> **Excuses are the language of the valueless life!**

If you value your job/career... you'll give it your all! You'll be on time! Prepared! Making a contribution!

One exercise that might be painful is to look back over the last ten years and see what your actions speak to you. Listen to your actions, and the voice of either encouragement from your conscience or the voice of correction, and see how your values have brought you to where you are.

I believe you'll hear more encouragement than correction, as you think back! And you need to celebrate your victories! It's evident you have a desire to be more than you are and to impact people with something that will make their life better. It's a good indicator of your values as you are investing the time to read this ebook.

What are some CORE VALUES that will help keep you on track:

HONESTY!
It's the Best Policy

INTEGRITY!
You never have to think of an excuse and apologize for a lie when you tell the truth.

RESPONSIBILITY! DON'T BLAME OTHERS! TAKE ownership of your successes and failures.

This one trait here when it comes to customer service will make you stand out from most in a crowded field of entrepreneurs.

FRUGALITY!
Save your money! Be wise with what you spend it on. Never forget you can save a dollar for a lifetime, but you can only spend that dollar once! Does what you spend your money on reflect your goals and values.

QUALITY!
You never have to apologize when you, your product, your life is the best you can make it. Some may not buy you or your product, but get over it... not everyone will like you, your product, or your life; and you may not be a right fit for them. They may not get involved with what

you and your business has to offer, but you'll never feel wrong putting your best out there that serves people!

A Giving Spirit - Cooperation!

Teamwork makes a huge difference, and the old sage said, 'you reap what you sow," or 'what goes around comes around." Have the value that you give your best to those you serve, and work with those around you. Know this—a generous spirit in a man will always receive more in return! It's a law!

WORK!

That is a great word, and the byproduct of work provides for you, your family, and establishes your family! Put in the time and hours it takes to make a difference in life and in your business!

TRAP #3: WRONG MINDSETS

You can have great specific goals, and values that even the Marvel Super Hero characters can envy, but if your mindset is wrong, you'll find yourself in a hamster wheel wondering why life never gets better!

Mindsets are your established set attitudes that you hold to, and the thoughts of your inner voice.

They are the inner voice you hear in your head that you play over and over to yourself. Your own voice that repeats in your inner conscience helps dictate your beliefs and the results you experience.

Years ago I had a terrible mindset! At the time my full-time income was derived from speaking engagements, and my calendar for the next six months was sparse with engagements. I was feeling the heat of too many months without the prospect of not much money. A friend that I greatly admired was talking with me, and the subject got to money. He asked me, "What's the first thing you think of when I say money?"

I never blinked or stuttered, but blurted out, "Money's hard to come by." It was something I'd heard from people all of my life say that and it had started to become the mindset that guided me. The second mindset after that was, "money don't grow on trees." That mindset had been pummeled into my conscience and started to become the steering mindset taking hold of my thoughts and life.

He said, "And that's the reason your schedule isn't full, and you are struggling financially... you believe money is hard to get!"

You know what? HE WAS RIGHT!

The number one mindset of Billionaires and Millionaires is there is more than enough money to go around, and to not only go around but to come to them!

I INSTANTLY changed the voice that I heard in my head, and the words of my mouth!

CHANGE YOUR MINDSET BY CHANGING YOUR WORDS!

Change the inputs you let into your mind. The voices you hear and the books you read.

Changing the words that you speak to yourself, and to others, is the quickest, surest, and best way to change a mindset.

I changed my constant speaking to myself right then, and I mean I talked to myself out loud and started telling myself, "Money comes easy!" and "Money comes to me!"

Would you believe that the next six months were the best six months I'd had in the previous 18 months! WOW!

Mindsets make an incredible difference in life and in the business you create for yourself! And if you are reading this, you want to be able to increase your life so that you can increase your income, so that in the long run your life can be the life you create, and not a life that just happens!

Mindsets to avoid:

DEFEATISM

Always saying to yourself, that if anyone is to win, it won't be you! This mindset alone will cause you to approach a challenge and believe that there is no use in the struggle, no use to fight, no use to defend or attack. You'll just accept what comes with every negative connotation and develop a pessimistic attitude of life and business. Defeatism will cause you to pull back and quit instead of charging ahead.

It's true you may not win EVERY TIME, but don't let it be because you didn't work and fight for the victory! Just the act of being in the arena pays dividend! You always learn more from your failures that you will your successes anyway.

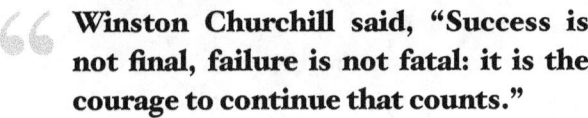

> **Winston Churchill said, "Success is not final, failure is not fatal: it is the courage to continue that counts."**

Mindset Change to say: "If anyone is going to win, it can be me, because I'm going to give every effort I can to the challenge and struggle in front of me, and in the end I'll be better for every effort I give!

'I AM WHO I AM' OR 'I AM STUCK WHERE I AM IN LIFE'-I CAN'T CHANGE

This mindset says, "my gifts and abilities are just what they are, and I'm stuck where I'm at," or "my situation defines who or where I am and I'm stuck!"

Nothing could be further from the truth! You can change! You can learn! You can adapt! You can overcome!

How many overnight sensations in music, art, business, politics, etc. do we discover only to find out later they had a twenty year process where they worked and practiced in obscurity to develop the talents needed to succeed? How many? Most if not all of them! No one comes to life with all the talent and skills needed to succeed in life.

There may be traits and tendencies that come natural to someone, but not one concert pianist, an accomplished musician, professional speaker, etc. ever demonstrated their ability without first giving themselves to practice and developing the gifts they want to be able to offer to others.

Brains and talent are your starting point, but never underestimate your ability to adapt.

The fact you are reading this means you were at one point illiterate. Really? Were you able to read a book when you were born?

Now you may have been four years old at the time when you started to learn to read but you worked on it, memorized words, applied yourself, and are now reading this report to help you in your life and business!

So good news! You have the ability to learn, develop, and change!

Develop a **'growth mindset'**! Develop a love for

learning and the impartation of knowledge that allows you to grow in every area of your life! Devour books, courses, programs, masterminds, videos, or whatever resources you find that will help you move in the direction of your goals and values. And do the one the needed–**CHANGE!**

Mindset Change to say: "I can do anything set before me, and if I can't right now I can learn how. Willful ignorance will not be a part of who I am; I have a mind and the capacity to learn what I need to succeed. And I'm open for instruction and change."

SCARCITY MINDSET

"I wish I could afford that," is how so many people talk to themselves, or they say, "I wish there was enough to go around."

I promise you something! If you want something bad enough, you'll figure out a way to get it. And I'm talking here within reason mind you. My Dad always encouraged me, "Never drive a car you can't afford to own, because if you like it enough, you'll figure out a way to get it."

That statement can be either a blessing or seen as a curse. If you focus on the first part only, you'll develop a scarcity mindset, but his emphasis was to make sure that my goals and values weren't forked off to something I wouldn't or shouldn't want in my life. Because you and I both do 'exactly what we want to.'

How many people have I met that say they don't have the money to purchase a program of learning or training, but spend thousands of dollars on other things, all the while complaining they don't have enough money? One set of friends of mine always talk of how they never have enough money to pay their bills, but every year they take a $12,000.00+ vacation to Disneyland... EVERY YEAR! Think about that. They don't have the needed money to pay their weekly bills, BUT they are able to put back $250 every week for Disneyland!

> **PEOPLE (YOU AND I TOO) DO EXACTLY WHAT THEY WANT TO DO!**

Scarcity mindsets see life as a pie that has only so many slices to go around, and not everyone can have a piece of the pie, and especially them. Are you like that? Do you have that mindset rattling around in your head?

Or they hear that there is only so much money to go around and there will never be enough paying customers for their business. You'll hear things like, "the market is saturated."

I once heard the story of a man who was offered a major stake into a hamburger chain for an investment of $100,000.00. He never had to move a finger, but would be considered a majority stake holder in a new chain of hamburger restaurants. He told Dave Thomas that there were too many hamburger chains now in America. There's not a need for another one. The name Dave Thomas gave it away didn't it. Wendy's is a major chain of restaurants, and at the end of the story the man, "See. I don't know everything, there was more than enough room for more hamburger restaurants."

Or they hear the voice speak to them that they aren't

worth what they really are worth, and so they price their business model so low they have to live barely getting by.

There's a story of Nikola Tesla, the man who invented the A/C current system and the power grid system all the world uses. The story says that Henry Ford had a problem at his factory and asked Tesla to find the problem. In a matter of minutes Tesla found the problem and marked the problem area with chalk; Henry Ford was thrilled to know the equipment that needed to be fixed and told Tesla to send him a bill. Tesla sent him an invoice for $10,000, and an indignant Ford requested a breakdown for the exorbitant bill. Tesla sent another invoice noting a $1 charge for making the X to distinguish the issue, and $9,999.00 for knowing where to put it.

Some say the story is a legend, but true or not, the principle is eternal! Tesla knew that the knowledge he had was worth more than just the mark on the broken piece of equipment, and he also knew the knowledge of Ford's need to have his factory operating was paramount to him succeeding. Ford's factory running was worth way more than the amount Tesla charged. Tesla valued the incredible knowledge he had and didn't let a scarcity mindset deter him from what he was worth.

A scarcity mindset will always require you to sell yourself short, and as the saying goes, "you're usually worth, exactly what you ask for."

Tune into the abundance that is in the world! There is always more than enough.

I've heard for the last 30+ years that the earth is running out of fossil fuels (oil) but new reserves are found each year! Could it run out? Possibly. But with the advent of new technologies more oil reserves, and the process to cleanly and efficiently extract the crude oil is being developed every year. One report in the 1990's stated that in the mid-2000's Saudi Arabia's oil production would begin to fall off due to lack of reserves... and in the last few years they have been drilling more oil per year than ever before.

The scarcity mindset will have live in fear! An Abundance Mindset will have you live with the hope that even when the earth does run out there will always be other alternatives.

Mindset Change to say: "I'm filled with abundance, and see that there is always more potential available to me, than there are disadvantages. My life is always prospering, and I'm always placing myself in a position to receive the most advantageous return for my efforts. The value of myself and what I offer people is far more value than I'll ever know to those I serve!"

BONUS PROTECTIONS: DILIGENCE!

Most people never realize the power of DILIGENCE! Or CONSISTENCY!

Putting in the time and effort!

Clocking in everyday!

Staying up late to do one more thing to accomplish your goals!

Trying one more time!!!

Make up for what you consider your lack of business or life skills and abilities by becoming the most diligent in your field!

Jack Ma, the founder of Alibaba and one of the world's richest men with a net worth of $36 Billion at the time of this writing is a diligent man! After college he applied for 30 jobs in his home town and was rejected at every one. He was one of 24 people who applied to Kentucky Fried Chicken, and 23 were hired, but Ma was not. He applied to be a cop along with four other applicants; the other four were hired and again he was not. He applied for a job with a cousin and scored much higher on the test; his cousin was hired, and he again was rejected. He applied to Harvard University TEN TIMES and was turned down every time. But he has the last laugh because of one thing.... He maintained his diligence and NEVER QUIT!

> **Winston Churchill is famous for telling the English people during World War II,**
> "Never, Never, Never Quit!"

Jack Ma once said, ""If you can not get used to failure — just like a boxer — if you can't get used to [being] hit, how can you win?"

It's diligence that causes you to get back up, stay in the ring, and to keep hitting and taking the hits!

Never let the hits of life or business keep you out of the fight!

Be diligent!

I hope this free ebook inspires you to stay out of the traps and pot holes of business so you can build the business and life you dream for yourself.

Bootstrap Business Academy is focused on helping you put together the right tools and resources that you need to accomplish your goals, your values, and to help you maintain the right mindset to tackle the next great adventure.

I want to invite you to be a part of the pre-launch of **Bootstrap Business Academy!**

Over the next few weeks I'll be following up with you on programs and trainings to help you launch your business no matter if you are just getting your feet into an online business or you've been around the block a few times.

Bootstrap Business Academy Podcast will be launching and using that medium to help you stay on track and inspired with everything we can to help you get over the humps of business and starting up and give you tools that you can put to immediate use! Be on the lookout for the **Bootstrap Business Academy Podcast** announcement.

My hope and prayer for you is that your greatest dreams manifest in your life as you pursue them with diligence! Abundance is for the asking… and together we are going places!

AFTERWORD

Thanks for purchasing "**3 Greatest Traps that Keep you Chasing Money, Instead of Making Money to Create the Life you Dream**"

I hope you have enjoyed this book, if you liked the book please take a moment and leave a review on Amazon, Goodreads, etc. Your reviews and comments are so appreciated.

If you'd like to learn what Chris is writing next, then take a moment now to sign up for Chris' email update by visiting his website at http://www.chrisvaughn.org

Also, if you find a typo, error, or such, take a moment and email me at mailto:chris@chrisvaughn.org and we will correct it. Also, you will be sent a free copy of our next book.

You can find out more about Chris by visiting his

ABOUT CHRIS VAUGHN

Chris Vaughn is a speaker, writer, communicator, sometime comedian, minister, and Pastor, who has also been a talk radio host, tv host, was a child on The Romper Room Show, and was a Candidate for US Congress. He is passionate about connecting with people to see positive change.

Chris is passionate about living a strong life, and influencing others, and you, to achieve your dreams, and laughing.

To find out more about Chris or to have him speak at your next event go to chrisvaughn.org

www.ingramcontent.com/pod-product-compliance
Lightning Source LLC
Chambersburg PA
CBHW051536240526
45471CB00020B/3020